W9-BGP-242

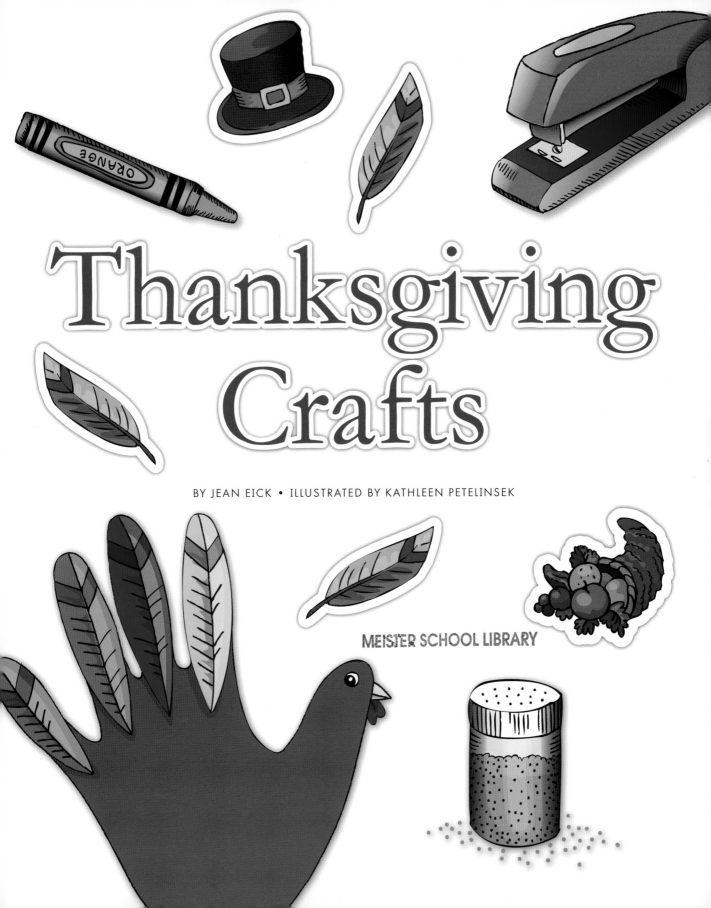

Thanksgiving Crafts

BY JEAN EICK • ILLUSTRATED BY KATHLEEN PETELINSEK

The Child's World®

Published by The Child's World®
1980 Lookout Drive
Mankato, MN 56003-1705
800-599-READ
www.childsworld.com

The Child's World®: Mary Berendes, Publishing Director
The Design Lab: Design and production

Library of Congress Cataloging-in-Publication Data
Eick, Jean, 1947–
  Thanksgiving crafts / by Jean Eick; illustrated by Kathleen Petelinsek.
    p. cm.
  ISBN 978-1-60954-237-5 (library bound: alk. paper)
  1. Thanksgiving decorations—Juvenile literature. 2. Handicraft—Juvenile
literature. I. Petelinsek, Kathleen, ill. II. Title.
  TT900.T5E352 2011
  745.594'1649—dc22   2010035475

Printed in the United States of America
Mankato, MN
December, 2010
PA02071

Table of Contents

Happy Thanksgiving!

Thanksgiving is a very special **holiday**. It's a time for people to be thankful for the things they have. It's also a day to remember the early settlers of the United States. Thanksgiving is always held on the fourth Thursday in November.

Americans have celebrated Thanksgiving for almost 150 years. It's a time to be with family and friends. Many people have a large meal with foods such as squash, corn, and pumpkin pie. Almost all Americans have one type of meat on Thanksgiving: turkey! But whatever people choose to eat or do on Thanksgiving, one thing is certain—it's always a day for being thankful.

Let's Begin!

1 This book is full of great ideas you can make to celebrate Thanksgiving. There are ideas for decorations, gifts, and cards. There are activities at the end of this book, too!

2 Before you start making any craft, be sure to read the **directions**. Make sure you look at the pictures too—they will help you understand what to do. Go through the list of things you'll need and get everything together. When you're ready, find a good place to work. Now you can begin making your crafts!

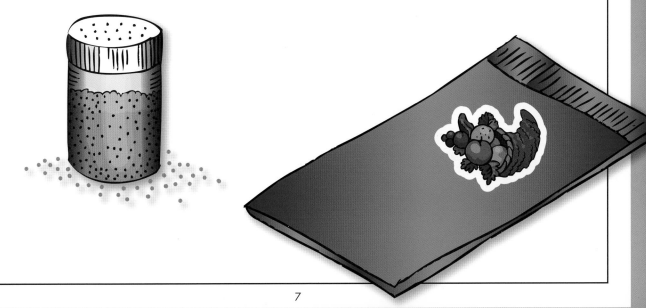

Handprint Turkey

These turkeys look nice on windows and walls.

THINGS YOU'LL NEED

Scissors

Pencil

Glue

3 sheets of construction paper
(one brown, one red, and one yellow)

Crayons and markers

DIRECTIONS

1 Put your hand on the brown paper. Spread your fingers and be sure to stick out your thumb! Use your pencil to trace around your hand.

2 Carefully cut out the shape.

3 On the yellow paper, draw a beak and cut it out. On the red paper, draw the turkey's **wattle** and cut it out.

4 The thumb of the handprint is the turkey's head. Glue the beak and the wattle to the turkey's head.

5 The fingers on top will be the turkey's feathers. Use your markers and crayons to make them colorful!

6 Use a marker to make the turkey's eye.

Paper-bag Turkey

A turkey is not just to eat on Thanksgiving! This turkey is made to be looked at and **admired**.

THINGS YOU'LL NEED

Brown paper lunch bag

Crayons and markers

Scissors

Rubber band

Tape

Newspaper

Brown pipe cleaner

Small paper plate

DIRECTIONS

1 Fill the lunch bag with crumpled sheets of the newspaper.

2 Put the rubber band around the top of the bag to keep everything inside.

3 Crunch and shape the bag to make the turkey's body.

4 Shape the pipe cleaner using this picture to make the turkey's head. Cut off any extra pipe cleaner.

5 Put the neck inside the bag end. Use your tape to keep the head and body together.

6 Draw a triangle on the paper plate. Carefully cut it out.

7 Use markers and crayons to draw colorful feathers on the triangle shape.

8 Tape the plate to the back of the turkey's body.

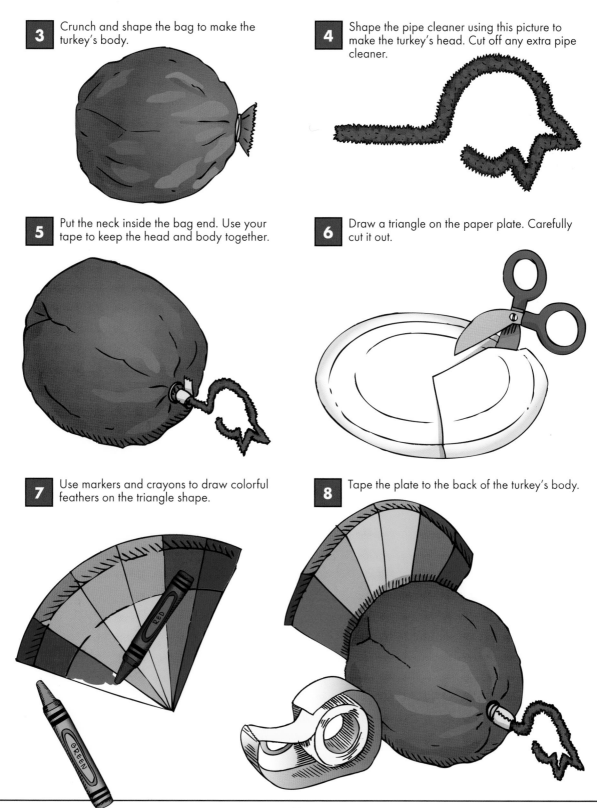

Decorated Napkins

Make lots of these napkins! Give some away and save some
for your own family's Thanksgiving dinner.

THINGS YOU'LL NEED

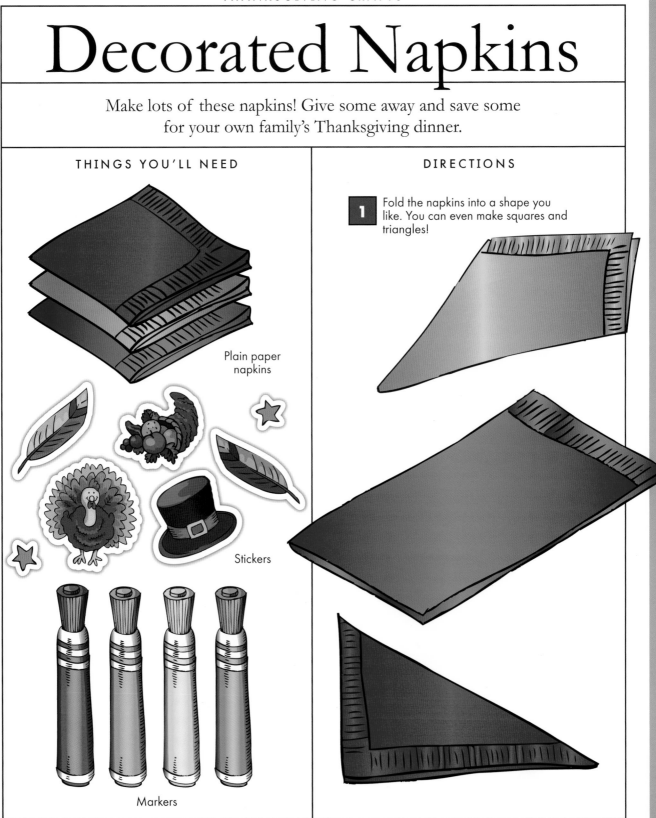

Plain paper
napkins

Stickers

Markers

DIRECTIONS

1 Fold the napkins into a shape you
like. You can even make squares and
triangles!

2 Decorate the front of each napkin however you'd like. You can make them all different, or you can make them the same so they match.

13

Napkin Holders

These fun napkin holders help napkins to stand up!

THINGS YOU'LL NEED

Scissors

Ruler

Stickers

Ribbon

Stapler

Hole puncher

Poster board

Paper napkins
(from page 12)

Pencil

DIRECTIONS

1 Use your pencil and ruler to draw a rectangle on the poster board. The rectangle should be 8 inches long and 3 inches wide.

2 Carefully cut out the rectangle.

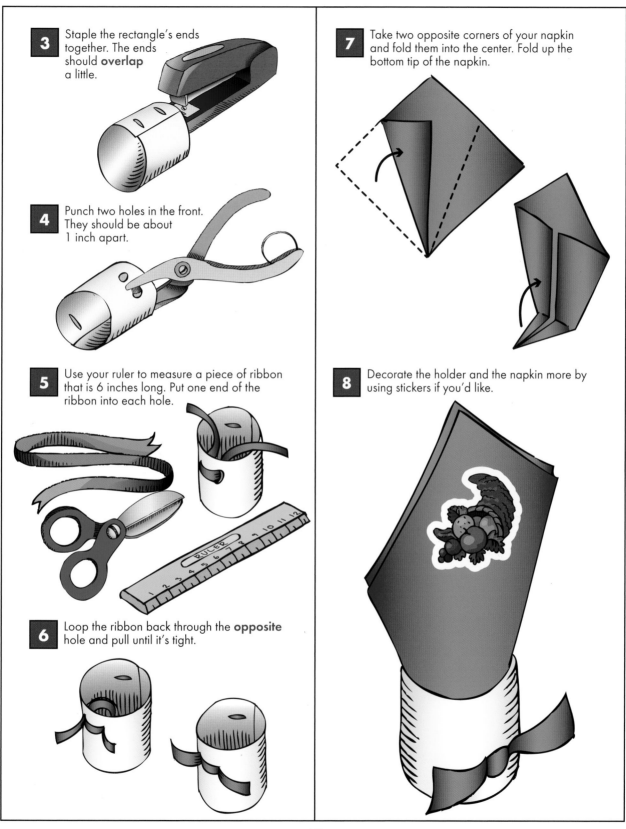

3 Staple the rectangle's ends together. The ends should **overlap** a little.

4 Punch two holes in the front. They should be about 1 inch apart.

5 Use your ruler to measure a piece of ribbon that is 6 inches long. Put one end of the ribbon into each hole.

6 Loop the ribbon back through the **opposite** hole and pull until it's tight.

7 Take two opposite corners of your napkin and fold them into the center. Fold up the bottom tip of the napkin.

8 Decorate the holder and the napkin more by using stickers if you'd like.

Table Runner

This gift will make Thanksgiving extra special for friends or teachers!

THINGS YOU'LL NEED

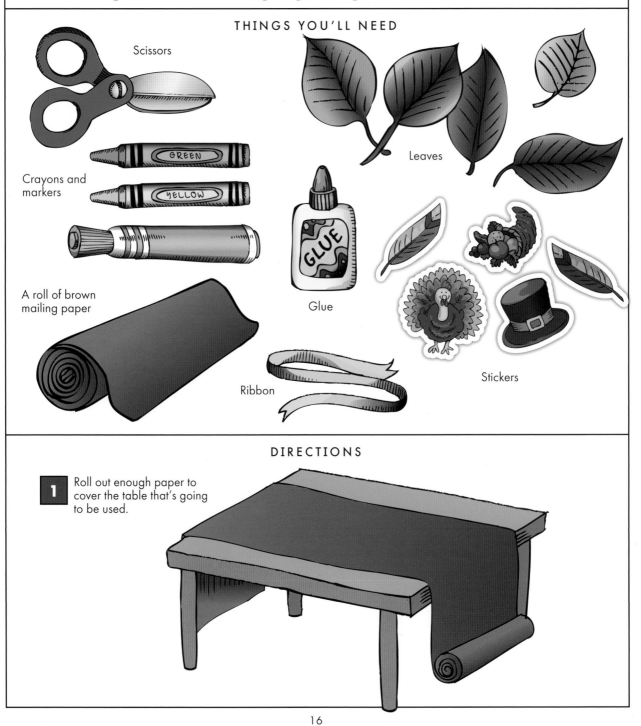

Scissors

Crayons and markers

GREEN

YELLOW

Leaves

Glue

GLUE

Stickers

A roll of brown mailing paper

Ribbon

DIRECTIONS

1 Roll out enough paper to cover the table that's going to be used.

2 Use your scissors to cut off the ends. Be sure a little hangs over each edge.

3 Decorate the **table runner** any way you'd like. Be creative! You can use stickers, ribbons, buttons, and even leaves from outside. You can also write messages such as "Give Thanks!" or "Happy Thanksgiving!"

Thanksgiving Cards

Thanksgiving cards are nice to give to your parents, grandparents, and teachers.

THINGS YOU'LL NEED

Scissors

Construction paper (lots of different colors)

Glitter

Glue

Ribbon

Buttons

Pencil

Crayons, markers, or paint

Stickers or magazine pictures

DIRECTIONS FOR CARD ONE

1 Fold a piece of construction paper to the size you want it to be. Folding once will make a large card. Folding it twice will make a smaller card.

2 Decorate the front of the card any way you'd like. You can use ribbons, buttons, glitter, and stickers—be creative! Write a message on the inside of the card. You can decorate the inside, too. Don't forget to sign your name!

DIRECTIONS FOR OTHER CARDS

1 You can make Thanksgiving cards in many different ways. Here are some ideas for making your cards even more special! Place your hand on the front of the card and use your pencil to trace around it. Now make a handprint turkey like on page 8.

2 For a picture card, use magazine pictures that remind you of Thanksgiving. Good ideas are leaves, big dinners, turkeys, and pumpkin pie.

Envelopes

You can make your own envelopes to fit your homemade cards.

THINGS YOU'LL NEED

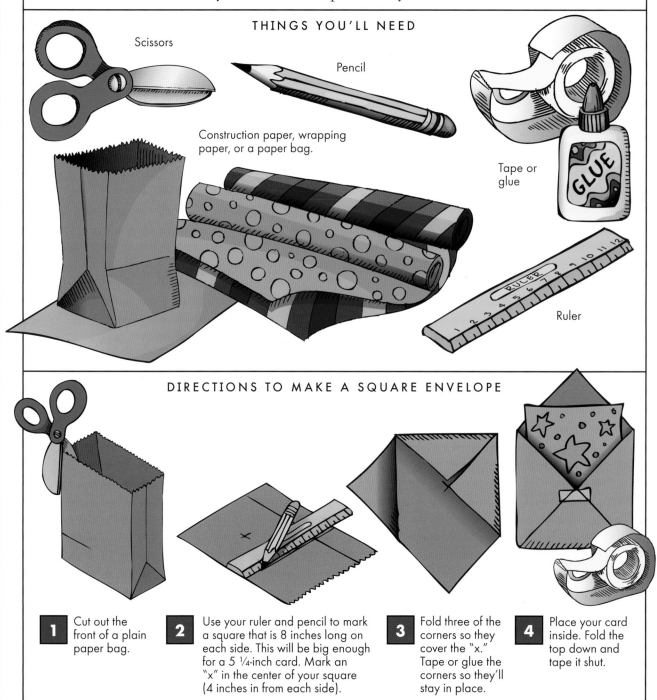

Scissors

Pencil

Construction paper, wrapping paper, or a paper bag.

Tape or glue

Ruler

DIRECTIONS TO MAKE A SQUARE ENVELOPE

1 Cut out the front of a plain paper bag.

2 Use your ruler and pencil to mark a square that is 8 inches long on each side. This will be big enough for a 5 ¼-inch card. Mark an "x" in the center of your square (4 inches in from each side).

3 Fold three of the corners so they cover the "x." Tape or glue the corners so they'll stay in place.

4 Place your card inside. Fold the top down and tape it shut.

DIRECTIONS TO MAKE AN ENVELOPE THAT'S NOT SQUARE

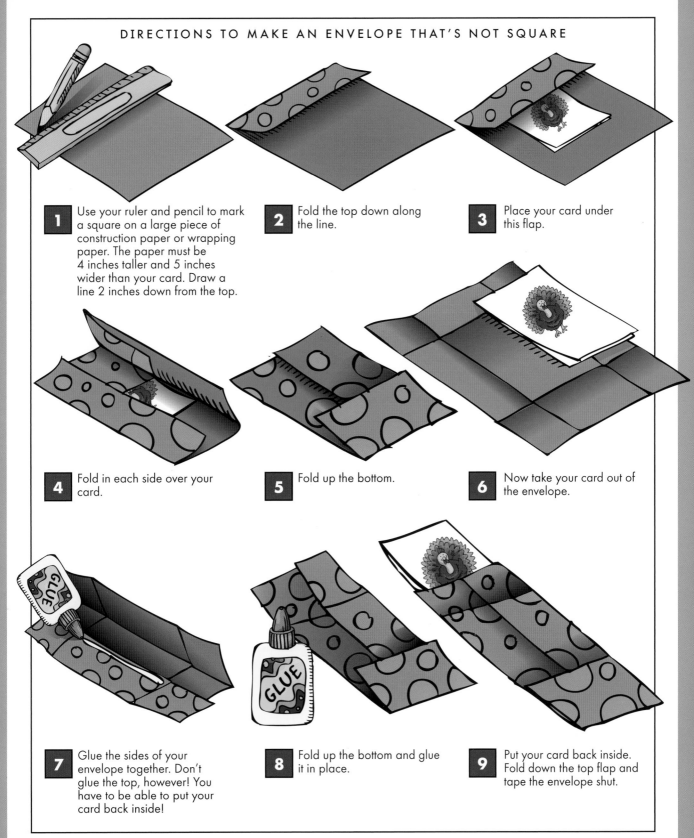

1 Use your ruler and pencil to mark a square on a large piece of construction paper or wrapping paper. The paper must be 4 inches taller and 5 inches wider than your card. Draw a line 2 inches down from the top.

2 Fold the top down along the line.

3 Place your card under this flap.

4 Fold in each side over your card.

5 Fold up the bottom.

6 Now take your card out of the envelope.

7 Glue the sides of your envelope together. Don't glue the top, however! You have to be able to put your card back inside!

8 Fold up the bottom and glue it in place.

9 Put your card back inside. Fold down the top flap and tape the envelope shut.

Activities

There are many things you can do with others to celebrate Thanksgiving. Here are some fun ideas.

1 Bake pumpkin seeds. Have an adult scoop some seeds out of a pumpkin for you. Rinse the seeds and spread them on a cookie sheet. Make sure no seeds are covering each other. Sprinkle a little salt on the seeds. Bake them in the oven at 200°F until they are dry and hard.

2 Help an adult make one of the dishes for Thanksgiving dinner. You can also set the table or wash the dishes after the meal.

3 Make a "Give Thanks" box. Decorate a shoebox with pretty wrapping paper. Then give everyone at the table a small piece of paper. Have everyone write their names and something they are thankful for. Put all the papers in the box. After dinner, open the box. Read the papers out loud for everyone to hear.

4 Have a table-runner decorating party! Follow the directions on page 16. Have everyone help with the decorating. Ask each person to write what they are thankful for on the runner.

Glossary

admired (ad-MYRD) When something is admired, it is looked at and enjoyed.

directions (dir-EK-shunz) Directions are the steps for how to do something. You should follow the directions in this book to make your crafts.

holiday (HOL-uh-day) A holiday is a time for celebration, such as Christmas or Valentine's Day. Thanksgiving is a holiday.

opposite (OP-puh-sit) When something is an opposite, it is completely different.

overlap (oh-vur-LAP) When something overlaps something else, it covers just a part.

table runner (TAY-bul RUN-nur) A table runner is a long piece of material that runs down the middle of a table.

wattle (WAH-tul) On a bird, a wattle is a piece of skin that hangs from its head or neck.

Find More Crafts

BOOKS

Ross, Kathy, and Sharon Lane Holm (illustrator). *All New Crafts for Thanksgiving*. Minneapolis, MN: Millbrook Press, 2006.

West, Robin. *My Very Own Thanksgiving: A Book of Cooking and Crafts*. Minneapolis, MN: Carolrhoda Books: First Avenue Editions, 1997.

WEB SITES

Visit our Web site for links to more crafts: childsworld.com/links

Note to Parents, Teachers, and Librarians: We routinely verify our Web links to make sure they are safe and active sites. So encourage your readers to check them out!

Index

ABOUT THE AUTHOR

Jean Eick has written over 200 books for children over the past forty years. She has written biographies, craft books, and many titles on nature and science. Jean lives in Lake Tahoe with her husband and enjoys hiking in the mountains, reading, and doing volunteer work.